My Dog's Recipe Book

Copyright © The Dog Journal Company
All rights reserved.

No part of this journal or any of our written book or works may be reproduced in any form without permission in writing.

This book belongs to _____
If found please call _____
Email _____

My Dogs Details

Name:
Date of birth:
Breed:
Colour:
Weight:
Microchip #

Insert Photo

Medical History / Notes

_____

_____

_____

_____

_____

_____

_____

My Recipe Book

Recipe   page #

My Recipe Book

Recipe   page #

_____

_____

_____

_____

_____

_____

_____

_____

_____

_____

_____

My Recipe Book

Recipe   page #

My Recipe Book

Recipe page #

_____

_____

_____

_____

_____

_____

_____

_____

_____

_____

_____

My Recipe Book

Recipe   page #

_____

_____

_____

_____

_____

_____

_____

_____

_____

_____

_____

_____

My Recipe Book

Recipe												page #

My Recipe Book

Recipe   page #

_____

_____

_____

_____

_____

_____

_____

_____

_____

_____

_____

Recipe Card

NAME OF RECIPE

_____

PORTIONS MADE

② ④ ⑥ ⑧ ⑩ ⑫

_____

FREEZABLE

YES \ NO

_____

THE DOGS REVIEW

☆ ☆ ☆ ☆ ☆

_____

VEGETARIAN ☐
DAIRY FREE ☐
LOW CALORIE ☐
GRAIN FREE ☐

_____

COOKING TIME

_____

PREPARATION TIME

_____

OVEN TEMPERATURE

INGREDIENTS & MEASUREMENTS

METHOD

| CALS: | CARBS: | PROTEIN: | FAT: |

NOTES:

12

Recipe Card

NAME OF RECIPE

_____

PORTIONS MADE

②　④　⑥　⑧　⑩　⑫

_____

FREEZABLE

YES　\　NO

_____

THE DOGS REVIEW

☆☆☆☆

_____

VEGETARIAN ☐
DAIRY FREE ☐
LOW CALORIE ☐
GRAIN FREE ☐

_____

COOKING TIME

_____

PREPARATION TIME

_____

OVEN TEMPERATURE

INGREDIENTS & MEASUREMENTS

METHOD

CALS:	CARBS:	PROTEIN:	FAT:
NOTES:			

Recipe Card

NAME OF RECIPE

INGREDIENTS & MEASUREMENTS

PORTIONS MADE

② ④ ⑥ ⑧ ⑩ ⑫

FREEZABLE

YES \ NO

THE DOGS REVIEW

☆☆☆☆

METHOD

VEGETARIAN ☐
DAIRY FREE ☐
LOW CALORIE ☐
GRAIN FREE ☐

COOKING TIME

PREPARATION TIME

OVEN TEMPERATURE

CALS:	CARBS:	PROTEIN:	FAT:

NOTES:

Recipe Card

NAME OF RECIPE

_____

PORTIONS MADE

② ④ ⑥ ⑧ ⑩ ⑫

_____

FREEZABLE

YES \ NO

_____

THE DOGS REVIEW

☆☆☆☆☆

_____

VEGETARIAN ☐
DAIRY FREE ☐
LOW CALORIE ☐
GRAIN FREE ☐

_____

COOKING TIME

_____

PREPARATION TIME

_____

OVEN TEMPERATURE

INGREDIENTS & MEASUREMENTS

_____

METHOD

CALS:	CARBS:	PROTEIN:	FAT:
NOTES:			

Recipe Card

NAME OF RECIPE

_____

PORTIONS MADE

② ④ ⑥ ⑧ ⑩ ⑫

_____

FREEZABLE

YES \ NO

_____

THE DOGS REVIEW

☆☆☆☆☆

_____

VEGETARIAN ☐
DAIRY FREE ☐
LOW CALORIE ☐
GRAIN FREE ☐

_____

COOKING TIME

_____

PREPARATION TIME

_____

OVEN TEMPERATURE

INGREDIENTS & MEASUREMENTS

METHOD

CALS:	CARBS:	PROTEIN:	FAT:
NOTES:			

Recipe Card

NAME OF RECIPE

_____

INGREDIENTS & MEASUREMENTS

PORTIONS MADE

② ④ ⑥ ⑧ ⑩ ⑫

_____

FREEZABLE

YES \ NO

_____

THE DOGS REVIEW

☆ ☆ ☆ ☆ ☆

_____

METHOD

VEGETARIAN ☐
DAIRY FREE ☐
LOW CALORIE ☐
GRAIN FREE ☐

_____

COOKING TIME

_____

PREPARATION TIME

_____

OVEN TEMPERATURE

CALS:	CARBS:	PROTEIN:	FAT:
NOTES:			

Recipe Card

NAME OF RECIPE

_____

PORTIONS MADE

② ④ ⑥ ⑧ ⑩ ⑫

_____

FREEZABLE

YES \ NO

_____

THE DOGS REVIEW

☆ ☆ ☆ ☆ ☆

_____

VEGETARIAN ☐
DAIRY FREE ☐
LOW CALORIE ☐
GRAIN FREE ☐

_____

COOKING TIME

_____

PREPARATION TIME

_____

OVEN TEMPERATURE

INGREDIENTS & MEASUREMENTS

METHOD

CALS:	CARBS:	PROTEIN:	FAT:
NOTES:			

Recipe Card

NAME OF RECIPE

_____

PORTIONS MADE

② ④ ⑥ ⑧ ⑩ ⑫

_____

FREEZABLE

YES \ NO

_____

THE DOGS REVIEW

☆☆☆☆☆

_____

VEGETARIAN ☐
DAIRY FREE ☐
LOW CALORIE ☐
GRAIN FREE ☐

_____

COOKING TIME

_____

PREPARATION TIME

_____

OVEN TEMPERATURE

INGREDIENTS & MEASUREMENTS

METHOD

| CALS: | CARBS: | PROTEIN: | FAT: |

NOTES:

Recipe Card

NAME OF RECIPE

INGREDIENTS & MEASUREMENTS

PORTIONS MADE

② ④ ⑥ ⑧ ⑩ ⑫

FREEZABLE

YES \ NO

THE DOGS REVIEW

☆ ☆ ☆ ☆ ☆

METHOD

VEGETARIAN ☐
DAIRY FREE ☐
LOW CALORIE ☐
GRAIN FREE ☐

COOKING TIME

PREPARATION TIME

OVEN TEMPERATURE

| CALS: | CARBS: | PROTEIN: | FAT: |

NOTES:

Recipe Card

NAME OF RECIPE

_____

PORTIONS MADE

② ④ ⑥ ⑧ ⑩ ⑫

_____

FREEZABLE

YES \ NO

_____

THE DOGS REVIEW

☆ ☆ ☆ ☆

_____

VEGETARIAN ☐
DAIRY FREE ☐
LOW CALORIE ☐
GRAIN FREE ☐

_____

COOKING TIME

_____

PREPARATION TIME

_____

OVEN TEMPERATURE

INGREDIENTS & MEASUREMENTS

METHOD

CALS:	CARBS:	PROTEIN:	FAT:
NOTES:			

Recipe Card

NAME OF RECIPE

PORTIONS MADE

② ④ ⑥ ⑧ ⑩ ⑫

FREEZABLE

YES \ NO

THE DOGS REVIEW

☆ ☆ ☆ ☆ ☆

VEGETARIAN ☐
DAIRY FREE ☐
LOW CALORIE ☐
GRAIN FREE ☐

COOKING TIME

PREPARATION TIME

OVEN TEMPERATURE

INGREDIENTS & MEASUREMENTS

METHOD

CALS:	CARBS:	PROTEIN:	FAT:

NOTES:

Recipe Card

NAME OF RECIPE

_____

PORTIONS MADE

② ④ ⑥ ⑧ ⑩ ⑫

_____

FREEZABLE

YES \ NO

_____

THE DOGS REVIEW

☆ ☆ ☆ ☆ ☆

_____

VEGETARIAN ☐
DAIRY FREE ☐
LOW CALORIE ☐
GRAIN FREE ☐

_____

COOKING TIME

_____

PREPARATION TIME

_____

OVEN TEMPERATURE

INGREDIENTS & MEASUREMENTS

_____

METHOD

| CALS: | CARBS: | PROTEIN: | FAT: |

NOTES:

Recipe Card

NAME OF RECIPE

INGREDIENTS & MEASUREMENTS

PORTIONS MADE

②　④　⑥　⑧　⑩　⑫

FREEZABLE

YES \ NO

THE DOGS REVIEW

☆ ☆ ☆ ☆ ☆

METHOD

VEGETARIAN ☐
DAIRY FREE ☐
LOW CALORIE ☐
GRAIN FREE ☐

COOKING TIME

PREPARATION TIME

OVEN TEMPERATURE

| CALS: | CARBS: | PROTEIN: | FAT: |

NOTES:

Recipe Card

NAME OF RECIPE

_____

PORTIONS MADE

② ④ ⑥ ⑧ ⑩ ⑫

_____

FREEZABLE

YES \ NO

_____

THE DOGS REVIEW

☆☆☆☆☆

_____

VEGETARIAN ☐
DAIRY FREE ☐
LOW CALORIE ☐
GRAIN FREE ☐

_____

COOKING TIME

_____

PREPARATION TIME

_____

OVEN TEMPERATURE

INGREDIENTS & MEASUREMENTS

_____

METHOD

CALS:	CARBS:	PROTEIN:	FAT:
NOTES:			

Recipe Card

NAME OF RECIPE

_____

PORTIONS MADE

② ④ ⑥ ⑧ ⑩ ⑫

_____

FREEZABLE

YES \ NO

_____

THE DOGS REVIEW

☆☆☆☆☆

_____

VEGETARIAN ☐
DAIRY FREE ☐
LOW CALORIE ☐
GRAIN FREE ☐

_____

COOKING TIME

_____

PREPARATION TIME

_____

OVEN TEMPERATURE

INGREDIENTS & MEASUREMENTS

METHOD

CALS:	CARBS:	PROTEIN:	FAT:
NOTES:			

Recipe Card

NAME OF RECIPE

_____

PORTIONS MADE

② ④ ⑥ ⑧ ⑩ ⑫

_____

FREEZABLE

YES \ NO

_____

THE DOGS REVIEW

☆ ☆ ☆ ☆ ☆

_____

VEGETARIAN ☐
DAIRY FREE ☐
LOW CALORIE ☐
GRAIN FREE ☐

_____

COOKING TIME

_____

PREPARATION TIME

_____

OVEN TEMPERATURE

INGREDIENTS & MEASUREMENTS

METHOD

| CALS: | CARBS: | PROTEIN: | FAT: |

NOTES:

Recipe Card

NAME OF RECIPE

_____

PORTIONS MADE

② ④ ⑥ ⑧ ⑩ ⑫

_____

FREEZABLE

YES \ NO

_____

THE DOGS REVIEW

☆ ☆ ☆ ☆ ☆

_____

VEGETARIAN ☐
DAIRY FREE ☐
LOW CALORIE ☐
GRAIN FREE ☐

_____

COOKING TIME

_____

PREPARATION TIME

_____

OVEN TEMPERATURE

INGREDIENTS & MEASUREMENTS

METHOD

CALS:	CARBS:	PROTEIN:	FAT:

NOTES:

Recipe Card

NAME OF RECIPE

_____

PORTIONS MADE

② ④ ⑥ ⑧ ⑩ ⑫

_____

FREEZABLE

YES \ NO

_____

THE DOGS REVIEW

☆ ☆ ☆ ☆ ☆

_____

VEGETARIAN ☐
DAIRY FREE ☐
LOW CALORIE ☐
GRAIN FREE ☐

_____

COOKING TIME

_____

PREPARATION TIME

_____

OVEN TEMPERATURE

INGREDIENTS & MEASUREMENTS

METHOD

CALS:	CARBS:	PROTEIN:	FAT:
NOTES:			

Recipe Card

NAME OF RECIPE

_____

PORTIONS MADE

② ④ ⑥ ⑧ ⑩ ⑫

_____

FREEZABLE

YES \ NO

_____

THE DOGS REVIEW

☆ ☆ ☆ ☆ ☆

_____

VEGETARIAN ☐
DAIRY FREE ☐
LOW CALORIE ☐
GRAIN FREE ☐

_____

COOKING TIME

_____

PREPARATION TIME

_____

OVEN TEMPERATURE

INGREDIENTS & MEASUREMENTS

METHOD

CALS:	CARBS:	PROTEIN:	FAT:
NOTES:			

Recipe Card

NAME OF RECIPE

_____

PORTIONS MADE

② ④ ⑥ ⑧ ⑩ ⑫

_____

FREEZABLE

YES \ NO

_____

THE DOGS REVIEW

☆☆☆☆☆

_____

VEGETARIAN ☐
DAIRY FREE ☐
LOW CALORIE ☐
GRAIN FREE ☐

_____

COOKING TIME

_____

PREPARATION TIME

_____

OVEN TEMPERATURE

INGREDIENTS & MEASUREMENTS

METHOD

CALS:	CARBS:	PROTEIN:	FAT:
NOTES:			

Recipe Card

NAME OF RECIPE

_____

PORTIONS MADE

② ④ ⑥ ⑧ ⑩ ⑫

_____

FREEZABLE

YES \ NO

_____

THE DOGS REVIEW

☆ ☆ ☆ ☆ ☆

_____

VEGETARIAN ☐
DAIRY FREE ☐
LOW CALORIE ☐
GRAIN FREE ☐

_____

COOKING TIME

_____

PREPARATION TIME

_____

OVEN TEMPERATURE

INGREDIENTS & MEASUREMENTS

METHOD

| CALS: | CARBS: | PROTEIN: | FAT: |

NOTES:

32

Recipe Card

NAME OF RECIPE

_____

PORTIONS MADE

② ④ ⑥ ⑧ ⑩ ⑫

_____

FREEZABLE

YES \ NO

_____

THE DOGS REVIEW

☆ ☆ ☆ ☆ ☆

_____

VEGETARIAN ☐
DAIRY FREE ☐
LOW CALORIE ☐
GRAIN FREE ☐

_____

COOKING TIME

_____

PREPARATION TIME

_____

OVEN TEMPERATURE

INGREDIENTS & MEASUREMENTS

_____

METHOD

CALS:	CARBS:	PROTEIN:	FAT:
NOTES:			

Recipe Card

NAME OF RECIPE

_____

PORTIONS MADE

②　④　⑥　⑧　⑩　⑫

_____

FREEZABLE

YES　\　NO

_____

THE DOGS REVIEW

☆☆☆☆☆

_____

VEGETARIAN ☐
DAIRY FREE ☐
LOW CALORIE ☐
GRAIN FREE ☐

_____

COOKING TIME

_____

PREPARATION TIME

_____

OVEN TEMPERATURE

INGREDIENTS & MEASUREMENTS

_____

METHOD

CALS:	CARBS:	PROTEIN:	FAT:
NOTES:			

Recipe Card

NAME OF RECIPE

_____

PORTIONS MADE

② ④ ⑥ ⑧ ⑩ ⑫

_____

FREEZABLE

YES \ NO

_____

THE DOGS REVIEW

☆ ☆ ☆ ☆ ☆

_____

VEGETARIAN ☐
DAIRY FREE ☐
LOW CALORIE ☐
GRAIN FREE ☐

_____

COOKING TIME

_____

PREPARATION TIME

_____

OVEN TEMPERATURE

INGREDIENTS & MEASUREMENTS

METHOD

CALS:	CARBS:	PROTEIN:	FAT:
NOTES:			

Recipe Card

NAME OF RECIPE

_____

PORTIONS MADE

② ④ ⑥ ⑧ ⑩ ⑫

_____

FREEZABLE

YES \ NO

_____

THE DOGS REVIEW

☆ ☆ ☆ ☆ ☆

_____

VEGETARIAN ☐
DAIRY FREE ☐
LOW CALORIE ☐
GRAIN FREE ☐

_____

COOKING TIME

_____

PREPARATION TIME

_____

OVEN TEMPERATURE

INGREDIENTS & MEASUREMENTS

METHOD

| CALS: | CARBS: | PROTEIN: | FAT: |

NOTES:

Recipe Card

NAME OF RECIPE

_____

PORTIONS MADE

② ④ ⑥ ⑧ ⑩ ⑫

_____

FREEZABLE

YES \ NO

_____

THE DOGS REVIEW

☆☆☆☆

_____

VEGETARIAN ☐
DAIRY FREE ☐
LOW CALORIE ☐
GRAIN FREE ☐

_____

COOKING TIME

_____

PREPARATION TIME

_____

OVEN TEMPERATURE

INGREDIENTS & MEASUREMENTS

METHOD

| CALS: | CARBS: | PROTEIN: | FAT: |

NOTES:

Recipe Card

NAME OF RECIPE

PORTIONS MADE

②　④　⑥　⑧　⑩　⑫

FREEZABLE

YES   \   NO

THE DOGS REVIEW

☆ ☆ ☆ ☆ ☆

VEGETARIAN   ☐
DAIRY FREE   ☐
LOW CALORIE   ☐
GRAIN FREE   ☐

COOKING TIME

PREPARATION TIME

OVEN TEMPERATURE

INGREDIENTS & MEASUREMENTS

METHOD

| CALS: | CARBS: | PROTEIN: | FAT: |

NOTES:

Recipe Card

NAME OF RECIPE

INGREDIENTS & MEASUREMENTS

PORTIONS MADE

② ④ ⑥ ⑧ ⑩ ⑫

FREEZABLE

YES \ NO

THE DOGS REVIEW

☆☆☆☆☆

METHOD

VEGETARIAN ☐
DAIRY FREE ☐
LOW CALORIE ☐
GRAIN FREE ☐

COOKING TIME

PREPARATION TIME

OVEN TEMPERATURE

CALS:	CARBS:	PROTEIN:	FAT:

NOTES:

Recipe Card

NAME OF RECIPE

PORTIONS MADE
② ④ ⑥ ⑧ ⑩ ⑫

FREEZABLE
YES \ NO

THE DOGS REVIEW
☆☆☆☆☆

VEGETARIAN ☐
DAIRY FREE ☐
LOW CALORIE ☐
GRAIN FREE ☐

COOKING TIME

PREPARATION TIME

OVEN TEMPERATURE

INGREDIENTS & MEASUREMENTS

METHOD

| CALS: | CARBS: | PROTEIN: | FAT: |

NOTES:

Recipe Card

NAME OF RECIPE

_____

PORTIONS MADE

②　④　⑥　⑧　⑩　⑫

_____

FREEZABLE

YES \ NO

_____

THE DOGS REVIEW

☆ ☆ ☆ ☆ ☆

_____

VEGETARIAN ☐
DAIRY FREE ☐
LOW CALORIE ☐
GRAIN FREE ☐

_____

COOKING TIME

_____

PREPARATION TIME

_____

OVEN TEMPERATURE

INGREDIENTS & MEASUREMENTS

_____

METHOD

CALS:	CARBS:	PROTEIN:	FAT:

NOTES:

Recipe Card

NAME OF RECIPE

INGREDIENTS & MEASUREMENTS

PORTIONS MADE
②　④　⑥　⑧　⑩　⑫

FREEZABLE
YES \ NO

THE DOGS REVIEW
☆☆☆☆☆

METHOD

VEGETARIAN ☐
DAIRY FREE ☐
LOW CALORIE ☐
GRAIN FREE ☐

COOKING TIME

PREPARATION TIME

OVEN TEMPERATURE

| CALS: | CARBS: | PROTEIN: | FAT: |

NOTES:

Recipe Card

NAME OF RECIPE

INGREDIENTS & MEASUREMENTS

PORTIONS MADE

② ④ ⑥ ⑧ ⑩ ⑫

FREEZABLE

YES \ NO

THE DOGS REVIEW

☆☆☆☆☆

METHOD

- VEGETARIAN ☐
- DAIRY FREE ☐
- LOW CALORIE ☐
- GRAIN FREE ☐

COOKING TIME

PREPARATION TIME

OVEN TEMPERATURE

| CALS: | CARBS: | PROTEIN: | FAT: |

NOTES:

Recipe Card

NAME OF RECIPE

_____

PORTIONS MADE

② ④ ⑥ ⑧ ⑩ ⑫

_____

FREEZABLE

YES \ NO

_____

THE DOGS REVIEW

☆☆☆☆☆

_____

VEGETARIAN ☐
DAIRY FREE ☐
LOW CALORIE ☐
GRAIN FREE ☐

_____

COOKING TIME

_____

PREPARATION TIME

_____

OVEN TEMPERATURE

INGREDIENTS & MEASUREMENTS

_____

METHOD

| CALS: | CARBS: | PROTEIN: | FAT: |

NOTES:

Recipe Card

NAME OF RECIPE

_____

PORTIONS MADE

②　④　⑥　⑧　⑩　⑫

_____

FREEZABLE

YES \ NO

_____

THE DOGS REVIEW

☆ ☆ ☆ ☆ ☆

_____

VEGETARIAN ☐
DAIRY FREE ☐
LOW CALORIE ☐
GRAIN FREE ☐

_____

COOKING TIME

_____

PREPARATION TIME

_____

OVEN TEMPERATURE

INGREDIENTS & MEASUREMENTS

METHOD

_____

| CALS: | CARBS: | PROTEIN: | FAT: |

NOTES:

Recipe Card

NAME OF RECIPE

_____

PORTIONS MADE

② ④ ⑥ ⑧ ⑩ ⑫

_____

FREEZABLE

YES \ NO

_____

THE DOGS REVIEW

☆☆☆☆☆

_____

VEGETARIAN ☐
DAIRY FREE ☐
LOW CALORIE ☐
GRAIN FREE ☐

_____

COOKING TIME

_____

PREPARATION TIME

_____

OVEN TEMPERATURE

INGREDIENTS & MEASUREMENTS

METHOD

| CALS: | CARBS: | PROTEIN: | FAT: |

NOTES:

46

Recipe Card

NAME OF RECIPE

PORTIONS MADE

②　④　⑥　⑧　⑩　⑫

FREEZABLE

YES \ NO

THE DOGS REVIEW

☆ ☆ ☆ ☆

VEGETARIAN ☐
DAIRY FREE ☐
LOW CALORIE ☐
GRAIN FREE ☐

COOKING TIME

PREPARATION TIME

OVEN TEMPERATURE

INGREDIENTS & MEASUREMENTS

METHOD

| CALS: | CARBS: | PROTEIN: | FAT: |

NOTES:

Recipe Card

NAME OF RECIPE

_____

PORTIONS MADE

② ④ ⑥ ⑧ ⑩ ⑫

_____

FREEZABLE

YES \ NO

_____

THE DOGS REVIEW

☆ ☆ ☆ ☆ ☆

_____

VEGETARIAN ☐
DAIRY FREE ☐
LOW CALORIE ☐
GRAIN FREE ☐

_____

COOKING TIME

_____

PREPARATION TIME

_____

OVEN TEMPERATURE

INGREDIENTS & MEASUREMENTS

_____

METHOD

CALS:	CARBS:	PROTEIN:	FAT:
NOTES:			

Recipe Card

NAME OF RECIPE

INGREDIENTS & MEASUREMENTS

PORTIONS MADE

② ④ ⑥ ⑧ ⑩ ⑫

FREEZABLE

YES \ NO

THE DOGS REVIEW

☆☆☆☆☆

METHOD

- VEGETARIAN ☐
- DAIRY FREE ☐
- LOW CALORIE ☐
- GRAIN FREE ☐

COOKING TIME

PREPARATION TIME

OVEN TEMPERATURE

| CALS: | CARBS: | PROTEIN: | FAT: |

NOTES:

Recipe Card

NAME OF RECIPE

_____

PORTIONS MADE

② ④ ⑥ ⑧ ⑩ ⑫

_____

FREEZABLE

YES \ NO

_____

THE DOGS REVIEW

☆ ☆ ☆ ☆ ☆

_____

VEGETARIAN ☐
DAIRY FREE ☐
LOW CALORIE ☐
GRAIN FREE ☐

_____

COOKING TIME

_____

PREPARATION TIME

_____

OVEN TEMPERATURE

INGREDIENTS & MEASUREMENTS

METHOD

CALS:	CARBS:	PROTEIN:	FAT:
NOTES:			

Recipe Card

NAME OF RECIPE

INGREDIENTS & MEASUREMENTS

PORTIONS MADE

②　④　⑥　⑧　⑩　⑫

FREEZABLE

YES \ NO

THE DOGS REVIEW

☆☆☆☆☆

METHOD

VEGETARIAN ☐
DAIRY FREE ☐
LOW CALORIE ☐
GRAIN FREE ☐

COOKING TIME

PREPARATION TIME

OVEN TEMPERATURE

| CALS: | CARBS: | PROTEIN: | FAT: |

NOTES:

Recipe Card

NAME OF RECIPE

PORTIONS MADE
② ④ ⑥ ⑧ ⑩ ⑫

FREEZABLE
YES \ NO

THE DOGS REVIEW
☆☆☆☆☆

VEGETARIAN ☐
DAIRY FREE ☐
LOW CALORIE ☐
GRAIN FREE ☐

COOKING TIME

PREPARATION TIME

OVEN TEMPERATURE

INGREDIENTS & MEASUREMENTS

METHOD

| CALS: | CARBS: | PROTEIN: | FAT: |

NOTES:

Recipe Card

NAME OF RECIPE

_____

PORTIONS MADE

② ④ ⑥ ⑧ ⑩ ⑫

_____

FREEZABLE

YES \ NO

_____

THE DOGS REVIEW

☆ ☆ ☆ ☆

_____

VEGETARIAN ☐
DAIRY FREE ☐
LOW CALORIE ☐
GRAIN FREE ☐

_____

COOKING TIME

_____

PREPARATION TIME

_____

OVEN TEMPERATURE

INGREDIENTS & MEASUREMENTS

_____

METHOD

| CALS: | CARBS: | PROTEIN: | FAT: |

NOTES:

Recipe Card

NAME OF RECIPE

PORTIONS MADE

② ④ ⑥ ⑧ ⑩ ⑫

FREEZABLE

YES \ NO

THE DOGS REVIEW

☆☆☆☆☆

VEGETARIAN ☐
DAIRY FREE ☐
LOW CALORIE ☐
GRAIN FREE ☐

COOKING TIME

PREPARATION TIME

OVEN TEMPERATURE

INGREDIENTS & MEASUREMENTS

METHOD

| CALS: | CARBS: | PROTEIN: | FAT: |

NOTES:

Recipe Card

NAME OF RECIPE

INGREDIENTS & MEASUREMENTS

PORTIONS MADE

② ④ ⑥ ⑧ ⑩ ⑫

FREEZABLE

YES \ NO

THE DOGS REVIEW

☆ ☆ ☆ ☆ ☆

METHOD

VEGETARIAN ☐
DAIRY FREE ☐
LOW CALORIE ☐
GRAIN FREE ☐

COOKING TIME

PREPARATION TIME

OVEN TEMPERATURE

CALS:	CARBS:	PROTEIN:	FAT:

NOTES:

Recipe Card

NAME OF RECIPE

_____

PORTIONS MADE

②　④　⑥　⑧　⑩　⑫

_____

FREEZABLE

YES \ NO

_____

THE DOGS REVIEW

☆ ☆ ☆ ☆ ☆

_____

VEGETARIAN ☐
DAIRY FREE ☐
LOW CALORIE ☐
GRAIN FREE ☐

_____

COOKING TIME

_____

PREPARATION TIME

_____

OVEN TEMPERATURE

INGREDIENTS & MEASUREMENTS

_____

METHOD

| CALS: | CARBS: | PROTEIN: | FAT: |

NOTES:

Recipe Card

NAME OF RECIPE

INGREDIENTS & MEASUREMENTS

PORTIONS MADE

②　④　⑥　⑧　⑩　⑫

FREEZABLE

YES \ NO

THE DOGS REVIEW

☆☆☆☆☆

METHOD

VEGETARIAN ☐
DAIRY FREE ☐
LOW CALORIE ☐
GRAIN FREE ☐

COOKING TIME

PREPARATION TIME

OVEN TEMPERATURE

| CALS: | CARBS: | PROTEIN: | FAT: |

NOTES:

Recipe Card

NAME OF RECIPE

_____

PORTIONS MADE

② ④ ⑥ ⑧ ⑩ ⑫

_____

FREEZABLE

YES \ NO

_____

THE DOGS REVIEW

☆ ☆ ☆ ☆ ☆

_____

VEGETARIAN ☐
DAIRY FREE ☐
LOW CALORIE ☐
GRAIN FREE ☐

_____

COOKING TIME

_____

PREPARATION TIME

_____

OVEN TEMPERATURE

INGREDIENTS & MEASUREMENTS

METHOD

CALS:	CARBS:	PROTEIN:	FAT:
NOTES:			

Recipe Card

NAME OF RECIPE

INGREDIENTS & MEASUREMENTS

PORTIONS MADE

② ④ ⑥ ⑧ ⑩ ⑫

FREEZABLE

YES \ NO

THE DOGS REVIEW

☆ ☆ ☆ ☆ ☆

METHOD

VEGETARIAN ☐
DAIRY FREE ☐
LOW CALORIE ☐
GRAIN FREE ☐

COOKING TIME

PREPARATION TIME

OVEN TEMPERATURE

CALS:	CARBS:	PROTEIN:	FAT:

NOTES:

Recipe Card

NAME OF RECIPE

_____

PORTIONS MADE

②　④　⑥　⑧　⑩　⑫

_____

FREEZABLE

YES \ NO

_____

THE DOGS REVIEW

☆　☆　☆　☆　☆

_____

VEGETARIAN ☐
DAIRY FREE ☐
LOW CALORIE ☐
GRAIN FREE ☐

_____

COOKING TIME

_____

PREPARATION TIME

_____

OVEN TEMPERATURE

INGREDIENTS & MEASUREMENTS

_____

METHOD

| CALS: | CARBS: | PROTEIN: | FAT: |

NOTES:

Recipe Card

NAME OF RECIPE

INGREDIENTS & MEASUREMENTS

PORTIONS MADE

② ④ ⑥ ⑧ ⑩ ⑫

FREEZABLE

YES \ NO

THE DOGS REVIEW

☆ ☆ ☆ ☆ ☆

METHOD

VEGETARIAN ☐
DAIRY FREE ☐
LOW CALORIE ☐
GRAIN FREE ☐

COOKING TIME

PREPARATION TIME

OVEN TEMPERATURE

| CALS: | CARBS: | PROTEIN: | FAT: |

NOTES:

My Notes

My Notes

My Notes

My Notes

My Notes

My Notes

My Notes

THE
DOG
20 ～～～ 17
JOURNAL
COMPANY

We hope you have enjoyed your recipe book. Please look at our other diaries, journals and guides. If there is something that we have missed then please let us know! We love to hear feedback.

Email us:- ihguide@hotmail.co.uk

Printed in Great Britain
by Amazon